Acknowledgements

I give honor to God who is still blessing me.
I also give a special thanks to Michael F., Kenneth and the editors.

This book is dedicated to my Father,
Coleman Wideman who was a military man,
loving husband, father, and a teller of stories, jokes, riddles, and sayings.

Below are two of his witty sayings that he had heard and passed along to us:

Truth will run all around the house looking for
it's shoes while a *lie* is out the door and down the street.
----
*If you are talking to a person more than an hour,
you are lying or repeating yourself.*

Positive

There is no reason- it's just that time.

TRUTH is a positive state of mind.

Table of Contents

What Goes Around Comes Around 7

Miracle. 13

Mood Swing. 19

Blindsided 25

Changing Habits 39

First Day Jitters 45

Friends. 53

Marriage (A-Z Story) 71

Is It Me?. 75

Poems For Everyone, Willie Pleasants' Collection. 77

Showcase: Works Of Other Writers 101

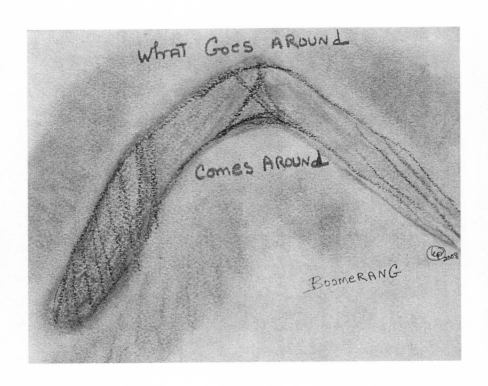

What Goes Around Comes Around

Hurry up to wait is the type of work that I do as a laboratory employee. The waiting rooms can go from packed with standing room only, to empty.

Last Monday, with no patients to draw, I retired to the soft padded barber like chair in one of the drawing stations to finish my book. Well, around eight that night, Beth, the X-Ray Technician, startled me as she entered my drawing stations crying, barely able to catch her breath. I handed her a box of tissues and offered her my seat, which allowed me to talk to her face instead of to her chest. I grabbed a stool and sat at attention. After a minute, her puffy eyes, face, and hair had become one color, red. Beth slowly glared at me and said with conviction, "For two years, I kept thinking he was too good for her- but now I know- he wasn't good enough."

I enjoyed good gossip. I knew it wasn't right but I didn't want to interrupt her. Beth blew her nose and continued, "I assumed Andy was perfect. I loved him and felt he loved me!"

"Is this Andy - your boyfriend?" I asked.

"He was my boyfriend," Beth said.

"Well, you'll be able to work it out, everyone fights."

"I don't think so…I should have never started a relationship with a married man."

He was married! I thought not wanting to seem insensitive. But it was hard to have sympathy for women who have affairs with married men. Beth must have read the expression on my face because she said, "Yes, he was married, but his wife cheated on him with his best friend."

"Did she really cheat on him?" I asked, with the vivid thoughts of my divorce. "I don't know, but that wasn't my worry," Beth continued. "His wife nagged him, wouldn't listen, never had much time, and didn't satisfy him in bed." As I listen to Beth, she hadn't display any expressions of guilt or shame. I heard that she was religious. I felt confused and a little uncomfortable because Beth and I seldom had conversations, especially of this magnitude.

"So! What if he was unhappy- that wasn't your problem," I said.

"I should have never pursued him, but I did." Beth continued. "Whenever he saw me at church he would cry on my shoulder, soon I made myself available."

"What!" I said laughing out loud without forethought of her feelings, "Men are very good at manipulating us with their lies. We allow them because we want to believe that the other woman is the problem!"

"Don't laugh," Beth said as she wiped her eyes.

"Sorry, I am not laughing at you, but at those women who think that they have platinum between their legs."

"I was a stupid fool," Beth said. As Beth talked about her relationship with a married man, it brought back memories of my breakup, but I was the wife. "You are beautiful and educated," I said hoping to console her. Even though I didn't approve, I felt badly that she had been mistreated. "Two years ago my husband left me for another woman." I said.

"Sorry, I didn't know," Beth said.

"Don't worry about me. I'm over him. I hope he and that hussy are very happy together."

"Thank you for listening. It was eating away at me." Beth said. So, I told her something my father told me, hoping to lighten the mood, or make her smile. "If it's eating away at you, it will kill me." It took Beth a few second before she responded, "That's funny," and we both laughed.

"In time he will be a distant memory," I said.

"Maybe, but I loved his three finger massages at bedtime," Beth said.

Suddenly, Beth was paged to do an X-Ray on her only patient of the night. While Beth was gone, I tried to imagine why she confided in me. Hello and Good-Bye, and an occasional how is the weather, was the most we ever said to each other. But, Beth's last comment had struck a nerve. My ex-husband gave… massages. Could that…? -Could she be? I just stared at the pages of the book. Thirty minutes later Beth walked back into the room with dry eyes and called me by my name. "Tamekia—I want to apologize for crying and unloading my problems."

"That's okay, who is this jerk? What happened?" I had to know the answer.

"Well, I don't think you know him but he's from South Carolina.... and to make a long story very short ...once he left her or maybe she left him, who knows, in any event he moved in with me. A year into our relationship his wife called asking for child support. I was shocked to find out he hadn't paid her. He wasn't helping me with my bills, so I asked him what was he doing with his money? He turned and told me to mind my business and stop nagging him! Can you believe that?" Beth replied.

"Get out!" I said as I held back my true thoughts. Suffocating from the details Beth had shared with me, it was hard to believe that this gossip had turned my stomach. "After that, he came home later and later," Beth continued. "It really should not have surprised me, but it did."

"No he didn't!" I said. The truth burned my insides.

"Well it ended when I informed him of my pregnancy. He told me that my pregnancy was my problem. He lost or quit his job and moved in with a new girlfriend."

"What!" Surprised to learn this bit of information. Beth looked down at her watch and realized it was time to go, and said, "I have to turn my machines off, but I learned a valuable lesson during that relationship. We always think the grass is greener on the other side, but when we get there it has these brown spots we couldn't see."

"Ya" I said, as I bit my tongue. It was hard keeping my emotions intact, but once her back was turned I felt uninhibited and said out loud! "Yes, girlfriend, you got what you deserved, cause what goes around comes around, Bitc...!"

Miracle

As the early morning mist disappeared, the revealed baby blue sky was captured and reflected in the nearby river. The sun's heat gave way to a seemingly ordinary day in Plainville.

Queen, a twelve-year-old girl, could be seen playing along the river with the other kids, but unlike the others, she possessed an extraordinary gift that had been dormant until…

Queen's stepmother called her in to run an errand. She rode her bike to Mrs. Simmons's Ma and Pa store. On her way a rumbling sound was heard in the distance.

Inside the store Queen heard the same noise but slightly louder.

"What is that noise?" Queen asked as she paid for the pepper.

Mrs. Simmons stopped, tilted her head, and stretched her neck so her right ear could listen.

"I don't hear anything unusual," she said, then turned and waited on her next customer.

Queen heard the sound again as she exited the store, but this times it was louder. Not sure if she was the only one hearing these sound, Queen stopped and asked one of the boys playing out front,

"Do you hear that noise?"

"What noise?" the boy asked.

"It sounds almost like thunder."

"No, you're crazy," the boy said as he walked away giggling.

Queen hears the sound again for the third time and became frightened and unsure of what to do. So, she instinctively rode her bike toward the church that was located in the opposite direction. She knew the elders would be there. She felt they would listen and not criticize, unlike her stepmother.

Queen arrived petrified and scared, but waited patiently in the hallway of Beulah Baptist Church. She did not dare interrupt the Bible Study Class as her upbringing taught her better. As soon as the class finished, Queen approached the pastor's wife.

"Mrs. Mabel, Mrs. Mabel, could I please talk to you?"

"Yes child, what is it?"

"I heard loud noises."

"What noises?"

"I am not sure," Queen said, almost in tears.

"Are you alright, child?"

"No, ma'am."

"Come to the office child," Mrs. Mabel said as she walked toward a room behind the pulpit. She stopped and gestured goodnight to the folks in the class.

"I don't think it's safe out there!" Queen said as she followed.

"Don't be silly, they'll be fine."

When they entered the office Mabel gave her water from the bubbler. "Child, why are you out this way alone?"

"I heard loud… noises…like thunder," Queen's legs were trembling as nothing she had said made sense.

"Calm down, drink some water and relax."

"But the thunder…"

"When did you hear thunder?"

"First at Mrs. Simmons's store getting the pepper for the rice. The last time I was on my way here."

"Child, where is your father?"

Queen had been so overwhelmed that she forgot to let her stepmother know of her whereabouts. She thought that her father would be furious, and the bike that her mother gave her would surely be the object of her punishment.

"He went out of town in his truck," Queen said.

Suddenly a commotion was heard in the pew. Mabel ignored the noise and assumed it was the church members that had stayed to bag the canned goods collected earlier.

"I see, but why didn't you go home?"

"My stepmother would not have believed me, so I came here."

"You waited over an hour for my class to finish?"

At that moment, the bumping and loud voices in the front of the church elevated to a level that could no longer be ignored.

"It's coming here?" Queen asked.

"No child."

"Something bad is happening out there, isn't it?"

"Now, now, calm down. We will get to the bottom of this."

The front door of the church slammed again and more voices could be heard. Mabel thought that was strange.

"Come with me child."

"Where are we going?"

"We are going to find out what all the ruckus is about."

Within seconds of Mabel and Queen reaching the front, a dark cloud covered the daylight coming through the windows rendering the people inside the church faceless. The strength of the wind intensified, going from a soft whisper to a loud howling. The heavy rain pounded against the rooftop like heavy rocks falling from the sky. The lightning's charge cracked the sky several times. The thunder was so loud the walls of the church vibrated, and everyone inside the church dropped to their knees.

"We are going to die!" a voice screamed from the crowd.

"It's the end of the world!" another voice said.

"Hold on to God's unchanging hand," still another voice.

"Is your house in order?" someone yelled.

"I cleaned it this morning," a stranger replied. Mabel snickered in spite of her nerviness, and so did a few others. Mabel said a silent prayer that the church would be spared.

As Mother Nature held her control, the moaning and groaning in the church got louder. Then, as quickly as she came, she went. The wind died down. The rain was reduced to light sprinkle. The sky became tranquil with bits of daylight returning. But for some reason the church swayed like a boat on the sea. With difficulty standing, the people grabbed onto the benches that just happened to be nailed down. Queen staggered toward her stepmother the moment she recognized her. Queen hugged her tightly with the hope that she would be forgiven. "What ya'll doing here?" Mabel looked surprised to see so many people.

"When Queen didn't return, I went to all the neighbors, and they joined me in the search," said Queen's stepmother. "We feared something bad had happened," one of her neighbors said. "I saw her riding her bike this way," the boy from the store replied. "So everyone came with me to make sure," her stepmother said hugging and kissing Queen.

"I'll have to put Queen on our payroll. She really brings out a crowd," the preacher said smiling.

A deacon yelled as he opened the front door, "We're surrounded by water!"

"The dam must have broken," the preacher responded.

"The building is floating! It's a miracle!" a voice from the crowd.

"It's not a miracle- the church was build to float by the last preacher. We thought he was crazier than a bedbug for spending the church's money on such foolishness."

Mabel looked around at the crowd, and then slowly turned and pointed to Queen, and said, "Queen is the real miracle."

Mood Swing

Susan leaned back in the deck chair with her feet barely touching the floor. She wiped the sweat from her forehead and said, "This morning I jumped out of bed headed down the hallway. My cat walked right in my pathway causing my foot to land him up against the wall. I couldn't stop. My mission was to get down stairs to the kitchen. Why? I don't know. But honey, I tell you, I thought I had lost my mind as I stood frozen in the middle of the kitchen."

You are not alone, I experienced that craziness in my late forties, and it continued right through my fifties," Ruby said.

"How did you cope?" Susan asked.

"Not very well, I remembered this one time I was exiting a mall parking lot when a guy tapped by bumper. I jumped out and called him all the four letter words I could think of and turned to his wife and dared her to speak."

Susan laughed, "You sounded like that strict Nun we had back in junior high who dared us to talk. Good thing you didn't have a gun."

"Yea, good thing," Ruby said as she opened the kitchen patio door. Inside were the sandwiches she had made especially for Susan's visit.

"Ruby, do you need any help?"

"No honey, you just sit there and take it easy, cause I wouldn't want to activate one of your mood swings, and have you kick me in the legs, just cause."

"Just cause, what?" Susan asked.

"Just cause you didn't have anything else to do."

"Don't be silly, I have it under control today," Susan said with an out-stretched pinky while sipping her ice tea.

"I hope so, cause we need to work on these neighborhood warning flyers," Ruby said as she poured more tea into Susan's glass.

"I can't seem to keep my mind on these flyers," Susan said.

"What's in this tea?"

"Tea juice," Ruby said.

We both laughed in unison.

"Oh, by the way, how's your cat?"

"My husband made sure she was alright, and they both avoided me."

"It was like that for me, too," Ruby continued, "I would come in the house yelling about how the house was a pig pin, and a bunch of animals must live here! I didn't really mean what I was saying, but I couldn't stop. My husband started helping me clean and cook, but stayed as far away from me as possible."

"Maybe we are going mad and should retire at the Mattapan Crazy House"

"You are crazy, that place is not there anymore. Condos and single family homes are on that land."

"Really- I guess I'm out of touch," Susan said with a look of despair.

"Don't feel bad you are not alone."

"That's not very comforting." Susan said as she tried to cope.

"Sorry." Ruby admitted.

"Let get back to these flyers," Susan said holding up the sign that read:

BEWARE OF THE INCREASING CRIME CAUSED BY THE THUGS IN THE NEIGHBORHOOD.

"Do you think the word thug is professional?" Ruby said.

"No, but thugs are not professional," Susan said as she grabs a glass of water this time.

"No more tea?" Ruby said

"No, I have to drive home." Susan said changing the words on the sign to read:

BEWARE OF THE INCREASED CRIME IN THE NEIGHBORHOOD.

"That's better," Ruby said.

Susan and Ruby went back on the deck in silence until the beautiful sunset faded.

Ruby followed Susan to the front door and said,

"We will have the signs printed tomorrow."

"Thanks for being empathetic today. It's mildly comforting to know that ninety nine per cent of the women our age are experiencing the same emotions."

"Only ninety nine and not one hundred?" Ruby asked.

"I think it will always be that one per cent who will not." Susan said.

"Really think so?" asked Ruby.

"Who knows," Susan said as she closed Ruby's front door and walked toward her red Corvette.

It was only minutes later when Ruby heard two gunshots. She rushed to the window and saw Susan running back toward the house holding something in her hand yelling, "I just shot that son of a thug, that I think tried to hi jack my car."

"Are you alright?" Ruby asked escorting Susan back into the house.

"Yes, I am alright."

"You poor thing!" Ruby said as she dialed 911.

"He's the poor thing! Cause it will be a long time before he'll walk again," Susan said calming down from her testosterone rush.

"Somebody better tell him when he gets out of the hospital; Beware of woman experiencing a mood swing, she is dangerous!" Ruby said, waiting for the police.

"Ain't that the truth," Susan said reaching for more tea juice.

Blindsided

Fresh out of college, at the age of thirty, it wasn't easy getting an interview with a top ten export company like Pearl Wear, but I did.

During my young adult years it was about me, until my mother kicked me out of her house. My girlfriend was about to do the same when I realized school was my best option.

At that interview, GQ was my look and a foot in the door was the gold. The Area Director, Steven Mann, told me that he expected the person he hired to improve the clothing profit margin. I vowed to increase sales by two percent each year to secure a job offer. It must have sounded good to them, hell it sounded good to me, if I could pull it off.

Sure enough, several days later they called to congratulate me. The company promised to give me a bonus each year my objective was met. I learned later that it was a false promise. With no reason to haggle, I was ready to do whatever it took to get the gold at the end of the day.

At my first official staff meeting, that month, I entered the boardroom with the best intentions to make a good impression. "Good morning staff my name is Juan Hernandez, the new Sales Director and my goal for this department is to increase our profit margins...." At the end of that meeting I felt like a fighter with a mindset to take charge and kick butts.

I thought that meeting went well, but seconds later, Jim, the assistant, walked over to me and looked me straight in the eyes and asked.

"Are you for real?"

"What do you mean?" I asked stunned.

"Do you actually believe you were hired for that?" Jim asked with a surge of anger in his voice.

"Don't be angry at me because you didn't get the job! The company must have felt I was better suited."

"Yes, they must have felt you were suited! You have no idea- for what!"

"Don't take your frustrations out on me!" I said agitated.

"You are absolutely right, I quit!" Jim said as he slammed down his note pad and walked away. Jim's action reminded me of my childhood friend Jose who would take his ball and go home whenever he got mad.

I though that Jim had made the biggest mistake of his career. Jim's leaving was the first of many dilemmas that I faced. I often wondered if Jim had stayed and told me what I later learned, would I have listened.

I couldn't let Jim's vacancy be a distraction. So, I exerted my authority and announced that a person from within my department would fill Jim's position. Mr. Stevens rejected the idea at first. After I told him it would boost morale, he only agreed if he could pick the candidate. That wasn't a problem at the time, but later I learned how relevant it was.

The following year the infrastructure of my department suffered lay-offs. I was forced to replace people who had ten years or more of seniority. I didn't believe the companies' accusations regarding those employees had any merit. Eliminating expert workers from a workforce was like taking the well-oiled joints from a perfect running machine and replacing them with ones that needed oil. It just didn't make sense.

I felt helpless, and then my father's words echoed in my ear, "Keep your mouth shut and do your job." So I did.

Of course, the company gave me the honor of being the axe man at the chopping block. I was not ready for that part of the job that rendered me a few sleepless nights.

"These lay-offs are not your problem," Steven explained, "we were going to let them go before you were hired."

Three out of the four people who received their pink slips went kicking and hollowing, but not Anthony. Anthony said something then that only makes sense now. Anthony was a slightly gray-headed man with hair that receded passed his ears. Spoke in a calm voice as if he knew this was coming, "You have no idea why I am being fired do you?"

"No, I was instructed to give the slips out," I said.

"I know every aspect of my job and yours," Anthony continued. "I have worked for this company for fifteen years, and for some reason I had become *incompetent.*"

"I am sorry, but it's nothing I can do." I said separating my thoughts from my actions.

Anthony walked out of my office and five days later he was found dead. The report never said what happened to him, but I hoped he died from natural causes. Unlike my only brother who died from a drug overdose. Maybe I should have at least tried to reassure Anthony that the lost of his job wasn't that bad. But how could I, when at the time

I felt it was. I had a family to feed and a mortgage to pay. It was just part of the job.

During the next five years I worked with, Bobby who had replaced Jim. Bobby was fresh out of college with energy to burn. He helped me update the system within the export business, which required long hours and numerous complaints from my wife.

"Juan, you have to find time to attend the kids' soccer games, just once before they get old," Jennifer scolded me one night as she relaxed in her bubble bath with a glass of wine.

"You have to take care of those thing," I said as the bed was the only game I had time for. I reminded her that my job was the reason we lived in an over priced home… the reason she was able to drive an expensive car. Especially when it was her desire to be a stay at home mother with a college degree and my need to be the breadwinner.

As my days drifted into weeks, and my months added up to years, it was amazing how time flew. Our computerized reporting system was completed. With less manual entries, I was able to spend more time at home with fewer complaints from my wife. My life had integrated into a weekday routine.

Before I knew it, Steven, was finally moving on, and it was twelve years later. I saw Steven's departure as a great opportunity for a promotion. After a peek at his salary, there was no way I was going to take his position.

Instead they recruited and hired Sal, on a working visa. Hell, I remembered how me papa struggled finding work in this country until he got his citizenship. All my siblings were born in the United States, papa made sure of that.

During Sal's first year I notice my bonus had stopped. At first I figured he was new and didn't know. But when it happened the beginning of the next year, I emailed Sal of that very fact. After about the fifth email, he called me into his office.

"Good afternoon, Juan, let's try to resolve this issue that you are having."

"Well, as I stated in the e-mail, I was promised a bonus the day I was hired, and had received them every year except for last year and this year."

"Well, I'm not aware of any contract regarding a bonus."

"I don't understand?"

"Well, Juan, I don't know what to tell you. There's nothing I can do."

"What do you mean, there's nothing you can do?" I asked. I saw Anthony's face flashed in my mind.

"Hold on, let me check and get back to you," Sal replied unconcerned.

"Yes!" I said, but I knew he wasn't. I walked out of his office, slammed his door, my Latino blood was boiling, but went back apologizing. I never want to cut my nose off to spite my face. In life it does more harm than good.

I went directly to Darryl the Director of Marketing for advice. He had been in the company much longer than I. I told him what had happened. Darryl advised me to check my personnel files. All reported activities regarding pay rates are in there. Also make sure it doesn't contain suspicious unauthorized reports.

Darryl told me what happened to his sister Billie when she checked her file. The supervisor of a department in which she applied for a position, had put a letter in her file with the comment, *he was not qualified.* It was obvious that they never interviewed her.

Deception with a professional face was new to me, so I went to check and happened to catch Pam, the Personnel Director, in her office.

"Come in Juan, may I help you?" Pam asked as she pointed to a chair.

"I'm confused about something," I said.

"Close the door, please"

"I was wondering-"

"I know just what you are going to ask me." Pam said as she interrupted.

"How did you know? ESP."

"I just got an e-mail from your boss."

"You did?" I asked. Thinking that that guy Sal works fast.

"I was going to have a talk with you tomorrow, but today is as good as any."

Pam continued, "Sal informed me that you were expecting a bonus."

"Yes, I was!"

"Well, I am sorry that Steven didn't explain what the rules were"

"What rules?"

"All bonuses are given to the Area Directors and not the Directors, but Steven was willing to share the money with you, for whatever reason, I wasn't privy."

"So you are saying that all those years, I wasn't entitled to those bonuses."

"Yes and no."

"Well, why would Steven do that?"

"I have no idea, but Sal has decided not to share his bonuses. It's really nothing you are I can do, that's the policy."

I left Pam's office shocked and mad as hell. I should have applied for that job, because Sal's salary plus the bonus was twice my salary. That was just not fair!

Darryl was my only ally. I spent more time in his office that last year than any of the twelve years at the company. I wasn't even sure if Darryl liked me, but for some reason I trusted him. Darryl had an honest conviction that bordered on bluntness.

"The way I see it, you have been blindsided," Darryl said as he looked over his glasses.

"I was tricked into believing a lie!" I said not being familiar with the word he used.

"See, it didn't pay to just keep your mouth shut," Darryl said.

"What does that mean?" I asked

"Oh, nothing. What will you do?" Darryl asked as I got the impression he wanted to say more, but knew he shouldn't.

"I have no idea," I said with my head in my hand.

A week later, me papa died at the age of ninety, and me madre had to come live in my home. I gave up the notion of looking for a new job until things settled down. The burden of pride was working against me. It was hard without those bonuses, but I had to make it work. I contemplated asking my wife to get a job, but what would my friends think? But unexpected relief came when my wife found a part-time job to get a few hours of separation from her mother-in-law.

The next year the company only gave small raises, but their profit margins were increasing by double digits. I had done my job well. It didn't help me as the gas prices were skyrocketing into space.

One day Sal approached me in the bathroom with a smirk on his face and said,

"Is everything alright, Juan?"

"Yes," I knew dam well he wasn't concerned or interested.

"I heard you have kids in college, money must be tight?"

I didn't know how to answer him. So, I left his words hanging.

The next year I was called into the personnel's office to meet with Sal. He had filed a formal complaint attacking me. He has reported my evaluation, *as improvements needed.* As Pam read the report, "… your reports lack important data, on several occasions you didn't meet your deadlines…." My mouth dropped to the floor and I imagined for a second that I had reached across the desk and punch him right in his mouth. He evoked feelings from my street fighting days. He would have been a good candidate for rock-em sockin robot with me at the controls.

"That is just not true!" I said as my voice elevated below a shout.

"Here are the reports that prove it!" Sal said with a Mr. Grinch grin.

"I don't know what you did, but those are not the reports that I submitted!" I shouted.

During the battle of words with Sal over perceptions and allegations, Pam had to pound on her desk with her paperweight to get our attention.

"Now-now, we need to act professional."

I left Pam's office frustrated, outraged, and devalued that this could really be happening, and to me!

The next morning I went straight to Darryl's office and closed his door.

"What's going on?" I asked demanding answers.

"In the next year Sal's brother-in-law's position is being outsourced and he will need a job." Darryl said sitting with his back facing his wall of degrees and awards.

"What does that have to do with me?" I asked.

"He will need your job."

"They can't do that!"

"Yap, they can and will."

"What!"

"They hired you."

"What!"

"Mack, the Sales Director before you, had a big fight with Steven. Once Mack confronted Steven about taking credit for his work, Steven lied to the president and said that Mack was lazy, insubordinate and should be fired. Mack tried to fight the allegations with no chance of winning because Steven had all his forged documents ready. Mack was blindsided, too."

"They told me he quit." I said.

"They always tell outsider that story."

"Man, you're joking?"

"You're not very smart," Darryl replied looking over the top of his glasses again.

"What do you mean?"

"He hired you, and has taken credit for your work."

"What the hell?"

"But for some reason he felt sorry for you and gave you half of his bonus money."

"Man, that's messed up."

"Sorrow to hand out bad news, but some of it you should have figured out."

"So, I was half screwed by Steven and now I'm being total screwed by Sal." I said, infuriated by the fact that Sal wasn't even a citizen.

"Well, welcome to the club. We got screwed out of forty acres and a mule. When we were emancipated, we were never truly free. Blacks are usually the ones getting screwed. Only this time it's someone else," Darryl said as he stood up with an injustice tone in his voice.

"So does that make you happy?" I asked, as I noticed Darryl was a much taller man than I.

"No," Darryl replied, "but its people like you who think that going along to get along will keep you with a job."

"What should I have done smart guy?"

"You should have asked questions, saw what was going on around you, and took your head out of the sand."

"I needed to feed my family!" I said angered at his accusations.

"Everyone needs to eat." Darryl continued, "You should have spoken up for people like Anthony?"

"What good would it have done?"

"You will never know because you did nothing."

"Well, I'm not a butt kisser!" I said.

"You said it. I didn't," Darryl said.

"I have worked hard as a loyal employee for this company."

"So did the people you handed pink slips to."

"I should be treated with respect," I said.

"We all need to be respected," Darryl replied as our eyes locked.

"I will not quit! I said with a voice of authority."

"It will not matter,"

"How could this happen to me?

"You are no different than the others," Darryl said as he released his stare.

I walked out of Darryl's office vulnerable and with reality calling my name. I didn't always agree with him, but I found I had to. Especially when he said, *"a smart man picks his battles very carefully. Sometimes the rights and privileges that are gained in human struggles by one group, often times benefit others."*

My wife reminded me that this wasn't my company, and without a union there were no guarantees. I kept copies of all my reports; even engaged in speaking out when it was necessary. It was hard watching my back, but it had to be done until I couldn't.

Sure enough, on my fifteenth year a pink slip reached my desk, they reported that my service was no longer needed. I pleaded with them to keep Bobby, they did but who knows for how long.

I felt like a wounded solider that fought for his country, bestowed his best years, and then released back into society without help. I stuck my degree under my arm and walked out of the building for the last time. My suspicions about the bonuses were never confirmed but I learned that Bobby was Steven's best friend's son.

Even though I expected this day would come, I still experienced progression of emotions that spiraled down much like a skydiver jumping without a parachute. Just before body and ground met he knowingly wished to change his mind, but couldn't.

No, I did not try to kill myself ... but that thought did cross my mind. Whenever I go past the building... I remember Anthony.

With the help of the church and my family, I have the strength to accept that when one door closes another door will open.

CHANGING HABITS

FAITH

It's not that which is seen
But that which it means
To have it, no man can stop your dream,
Only slow it up with steam.

God knows your name,
he can help change your game.
So, don't be depress, it temporary at best,
"Faith" is the answer to your stress.

CHANGING HABITS

"Charlie, Charlie," she whispered as the sweet echoing sound filled the room. Her slender legs and arms played musical sounds with my body, and I allowed it. Each movement of her buttock caused a tantalizing powerful pressure to build.

"Slow-er, slow-er," were the words that floated from my tongue into her ear. An uncontrollable sensation that escalated into a climactic force that struck every nerve, and I loved it!

"Charlie, Charlie," she whispered again as she was in control, except for that last second when I bellowed out a loud moan, releasing an overpowering urge that curled my toes. At that precise moment my juices exploded into a shield that resided within her. Our fireworks must have ended at the same time, because she collapsed and slowly rolled off. Side by side we were soaking from the aftermath. In spite of the latex, it was a distorted scene from the mirrors above.

I propped my pillow against the head of the bed, and closed my eyes to mentally inhale a smoked flavored Winston. I leaned my head back to slowly exhale small donut shape rings. It truly was a cigarette flashback after seven years of being smoke free.

When Margaret's cell phone rang, I jumped up and stood beside the bed as my heart raced. She flipped it opened on the fourth charm and said,

"Hello Hon, you woke me up from a wonderful nap."

I went into the bathroom leaving Margaret to deal with her paradox of a marriage, while I dealt with the cramps in my stomach. The pains I felt were directly related to an internal struggle of fear due to my involvements in these types of relationships.

I will never forget the night my pastor came home early, snuck into his bedroom not wanting to wake his wife, pulled back the cover and found us. I vacated that house barely escaping with my life and a large gash across my right shoulder. It took a year to heal.

A man with a knife didn't surprise me, nor was it the first time a husband chased me out of his house, but the fact that a pastor cut me was shocking.

"You are a dead man!" He yelled as he chased me two miles down the block.

So, I had to put distance between him, his church, and his wife. One of my Alabama cousins told me later that I should be thankful to be alive, "southerners are gentile-men, who could have ended your life. "

I turned the shower water on as hot as I could stand, jumped in, and attempted to wash away the last thoughts of Margaret and the Pastor.

As Margaret hung up her cell phone, she joined me in the bathroom.

"Bob expects to see you at work on Monday," Margaret said as she refreshed her make-up.

"Why?" I asked stepping out of the shower.

"You are our best Agent," Margaret said, "Bob is having an office party in your honor."

I looked at Margaret and asked,

"How did we get to this point?"

"We were both lonely and -," Margaret started to say.

"Stop!" I replied, "I was lonely, but you wanted revenge."

Again, I left Margaret's townhouse that night, satisfied by the only thing that sustained our relationship. Margaret was never going to leave her husband, and I knew it.

The day of the party Margaret walked into my office, closed the door and handed me another gift.

"Hon, our next rendezvous?" Margaret asked.

"Come-on" I said as I reluctantly received the gift.

"Sorry, I really didn't mean it that way."

"This had to end!" I said as my words were slowly losing their value.

"Well, if you are that unhappy, just leave. I will find someone else."

"You are an arrogant..."

"I 'm not arrogant! But - you- you like living dangerously!" Margaret said as she pushed back the small pieces of gray hair that nestled around her edges.

"You don't know me," I said, "besides, you have the lavish lifestyle."

"Yes, because I stay in this camouflage of marriage."

"Then leave!"

Something come over Margaret and her body froze, she went into a trance when a soft voice emerged, "I really loved him, he cheated on me." Margaret's body joisted. Then she spoke in her normal voice, "I refuse to be poor!"

"Margaret, are you okay?" I asked.

"I am fine! Just fine!"

"Are you afraid of what Bob might do if he catches you cheating?" I asked.

"Nothing! He will do nothing to me, but you need to worry about what he will do to you." Margaret said in a matter of fact way.

"What did that mean?" I asked. She just smiled walking out the door.

During the party, Margaret's husband, Bob, pulled me aside and said,

"Congratulation James! Margaret and I are extremely pleased with your performance this year."

"Thank you." I said.

"My wife worked hard putting this party together. I love her. I can not imagine life without her."

As I walked away from Bob, I couldn't help wondering if he knew.

Cheryl, a co-worker, grabbed my arm and escorted me into her office and said, "Several years ago there was a rumor that Margaret's husband found her cheating? He took her back, but the man was never seen again."

"Who told you that?" I asked

"I can't say."

Bob's words were compelling but Cheryl's statement couldn't be ignored. I loved my job, enjoyed being appreciated, but didn't want to be fired. Nor did I want to get killed in the name of a loveless affair. *I had to change.*

I later learned that Bob had an affair that resulted with a child. A baby that Margaret's body could never create. Bob's guilt allowed Margaret to have sex outside their marriage.

Sadly, I worried about Margaret's life instead of my own. My mother had said to me before she died, "As a so called church man you need to make Godly habits a priority." I knew in an adulterous affair there are too many, ifs, ands, buts, and no safe outs.

A year later, Margaret came into my office excited about introducing, Jim, the newest employee. Shaking Jim's hand I surprisingly noticed his watch; it was the same type of watch she had given me two years earlier. *Some people never change.*

First Day Jitters

The sound of the ambulance's siren caused my hands to shake. It was time to face my fears or go home. I hurried out of the café and down the hallway toward the emergency ward. I wanted to prove to the world that I could be a good intern and someday a great doctor. Mom didn't think it was such a great idea at the age of forty, but dad said to go for it! So there I was finally facing the world with all my idiosyncrasies.

In a rush to prove myself, I tripped and dropped the last piece of tuna fish sandwich trying to hold it and a can of soda. Imagine me down on my knees cleaning up my mess instead of my kids; it felt bazaar. I had to hurry if I was going to save my first patient.

"Move it! Get out of the way people!" I heard the triage nurse yelling as he directed the two medics with their patient to the first available room.

I dashed in just as the medics were transferring the patient from the gurney to a hospital bed.

"This young male had an accident while riding his bike along the Charles River," one of the medic said.

So, I figured this would be a perfect opportunity to demonstrate my intelligence as an intern. I walked over to the young male's bedside, released the straps on the brace that surrounded his leg. All I wanted to do was examine it. Then suddenly, the patient yelled out an agonizing scream, which scared me.

Within seconds, Martha, the head nurse, entered the room with a tailwind that pushed me against the wall.

"Pull his leg so that we can reset his fracture!"

With feelings of inadequacy, I did as I was told.

"Who's teaching classes at that medical school?" Martha asked, as I envisioned protruding red horns from her head, and green daggers flying from her tongue directed at me. "You are old enough to know better than to remove a splint from a freshly broken femur."

"Sorry," I muttered, and like a wounded dog, I tucked my head down and scurried out of the room. I wasn't thinking.

Dr. Taylor, the resident doctor spotted me in the hallway heading toward the soda machine, and said, "Dr. Mann, next time, read the patient's information sheet."

"Yes Dr. Taylor," I said as I walked away.

"You-you no fix me," the janitor said as he walked pass me laughing.

"It happens to the best of us," a student nurse said joining me in the walk to the soda machine.

What happened to confidentiality, are we not in a hospital? I really need to get my act together because one mistake is one too many. I cannot let this dream become a failure, like my twenty-year marriage.

As I finished my soda and headed back to the nurses' station I heard my name paged, "Dr. Mann-paging Dr. Mann."

"Yes, Martha?" I asked from behind her. She jumped right out of her clogs.

"Don't do that again," Martha demanded.

"Sorry," I apologized because it wasn't nice. It was just an unconscious reflex from my childish days.

"Dr. Mann! We have a mother with her six-year-old child in room 2. The child is having difficulty swallowing, and her temperature is 103," Martha said.

This time I read the chart and than cautiously examined my second patient. The child's fever and sore throat was consistent with a need to do a throat culture.

"Martha, can you do a throat culture and take it to the lab?" I asked.

Martha paused and tossed me a culture swab.

Martha asked the other nurse as they walked away laughing. "Did she really expect me to do it?"

I didn't particularly appreciate being the brunt of people banter, but it seemed to be part of this job.

Half-hour later the Rapid Test came back positive for Streptococcus. A prescription was written and the child was discharged. Second case resolved – next!

With several throats examined and a few urine infections (UTI) treated, I was back in charge! With a smile, and ideals of grandeur intact, I was back to healing the sick. For the first time that night, I felt going back to medical school was the right choice.

Twelve hours into the night shift, I could have sworn the nurse behind a curtain was telling a patient, "Keep that thing in your pants and zip up."

If I hadn't been so tired, I would have sneaked a peek.

"Paging Dr. Mann—Paging Dr. Mann, please report to the nurses' station."

"Ok - Ok, coming you…. in the backside."

"Dr. Mann you have a forty or fifty year old male, John Doe, in room 4. His temperature is 98.6; blood pressure 190/100." Martha said.

"That's strange- there was a Jane Doe in room 8 earlier, are they related?" a student nurse asked.

"No silly," I said as I laughed, "Administration issues wristbands with the name John or Jane Doe, to any unidentified patient."

"Oh, I really have a lot to learn," she said.

"We both do," I replied.

As I walked into room 4, the odor of alcohol permeated that space. It was impossible to stay more than a few minutes without intervals of fresh air.

"John Doe was found at the Hilton Red Hotel. The bellboy who found him said that John complained of abdominal pains just before he collapsed," the ambulance's driver reported.

After reviewing his chart, I filled a requisition requesting the Laboratory Technician to draw a battery of tests. While I waited for John Doe's results, a code 99 in the next room drew my attention.

I walked into the room as the nurse read the report. "A twenty-five years old male gunshot patient. His girlfriend drove him in. She said they had argued, he pulled a knife on her and she shot him with the very gun he had given her to keep. The girlfriend told the police she didn't mean to shoot but only scare him." I guess it was true about strange things happening on the *graveyard shift*.

After a few hours, John Doe's blood results came back normal, except for his alcohol level and a few other barbiturates. That explained why he was semiconscious, but it didn't explain his occasional moans and groans and holding his lower abdomen area. I had no clue, so I went to Dr. Taylor for advice.

"Did you do a rectum exam to rule out any problems there?" he asked.

"Must I?" This shouldn't have been a problem as many diapers I changed in my lifetime. But it was.

"Yes, and you will be a better doctor for it," Dr. Taylor said never looking up from his paperwork.

"Somehow I knew you were going to say that," I am sure John Doe would have preferred a male doctor working on his rear end. I did it, but I am yet to see how better for it I will be. I filled out a requisition and sent it to the Radiology Department requesting an X-Ray. When the films came back, I called Dr. Taylor for a consultation. I wanted him to look at the films to confirm my suspicion.

John Doe was taken into a surgical room. I could not believe my eyes nor could Dr. Taylor. We both looked at each other in sheer amazement. There seemed to be no ends to this round object that Dr. Taylor pulled from John Doe's anus.

"Never in all my years of practice," Dr. Taylor said.

At first I thought it was a long, stick of salami, but the Histology Lab. told us later that it was a large candle.

"Hey, this gives new meaning to twelve inches and hard as a rock," another Intern whispered as he leaned over my shoulder.

Finally my shift had ended. Thank you God! I had survived.

As I walked pass the front desk, I heard the janitor tell the secretary, "Last night, this guy came into the E.R. in this Armando suit, with Stacio Adams shoes… they pulled this…from his..!"

I smiled because the torch had been passed, and John was now the blunt of their jokes. As the morning sunlight touched my face, I noticed that my hands were not shaking.

FRIENDS

A teardrop grew
The moment I knew

You were part of
A dream come true

Thank you again
For making me feel

LIKE A FRIEND.

This story continues from my first book **...Ain't That The Truth** by Willie Pleasants.

FRIENDS

Chapter One

I recalled the last time Betty and Sam had sat across from each other. They had lost their only daughter, Mary Ellen. Sam was speechless after learning that he was Mary Ellen's father. Betty had us believing that Mary Ellen was April's daughter. With Mary Ellen's beautiful mahogany complexion and bone structure resembling April rather than Betty, we believed her. At the funeral Betty found that she had to tell us the truth or April would have. Sam hadn't spoken to Betty since.

Until six months ago, I thought I had gotten rid of all my ill will toward Betty, but my subconscious exposed my true feelings in a dream. In that dream, Betty came at me with a left hook, which brought me to my knees. As Betty turned to walk away, I grabbed the tail of her dress. It ripped as I pulled her to the floor. As we wrestled back and forth, Betty's hand grabbed my hair for support. Her fingers held onto a piece of weave that soon let go. I went for her head and my hand came away with her wig. Our fight had the makings of a bar room brawl with flying hair, hat and dress. From the corner of my eye, I saw shadows of people gathering, which made Betty and I the main attraction. We clawed at each other like animals. An age-old vendetta no one dared stop.

"Cat fight, cat fight!" yelled a man. The crowd stood with their bright eyes of amusement waiting to announce a winner.

"Finish her off, and be done!" yelled a female. As I gained enough strength, I crawled onto Betty's back. I lassoed her legs and arms together like a cowgirl at a rodeo. Betty kicked and screamed unable to get free. I had finally won! I pounded on my chest and made that – that sounds only *Jane* could make after capturing an attacker. "Queen of the jungle!" everyone roared as my alarm clock buzzed. I jumped out of bed with a smile on my face.

Chapter Two

A month later at home in Detroit, I was surfing the web. I was looking to purchase two commercial properties, one in Detroit and one in Boston, when the phone rung.

"Hello," Sam said.

"How are you?"

"Not so good."

"Sam, what happen to the investigation into Mary Ellen's death?"

"I don't know! Talk about something else?"

"Well, I'm getting married."

"You have finally down-graded your knight in shining armor?"

"I never thought my expectations were high." I knew Sam was kidding because he was like a brother.

"When is the wedding?"

"This June, and I am inviting Shanda, therefore, I have to invite Betty. It wouldn't be right if I don't."

"*Now* you are worried about doing the right thing?" Sam asked.

"Yes, I learned that running away from problems doesn't solve them."

"You can invite whomever you please."

"I know, but you have to come to give me away."

"It will be an honor to do it for you."

"Thank you, Sam."

Chapter Three

A week later in my kitchen, my bare feet felt good against the marble floor. I had a cup of tea reflecting on how I met Jim, my fiancé.

Three years ago, I had been sitting on a delayed flight back to Detroit. I didn't feel like having a conversation with anyone. The owner of one of the properties had neglected to inform me of a lien that another company had against the building that I was purchasing. I had only discovered it during the lien certificate search. I was furious.

An announcement over the plane's intercom system stated that high winds were the reason they hadn't yet taken off. Go figure! So I stuck my head in a book with the hopes of being inconspicuous. It wasn't easy, because I was one of twenty passengers on a crop duster.

"So are you married?" the pilot asked.

"Are you talking to me?" I asked

"Yes, pretty lady."

"No, if you must know."

"Do you have any children?"

"No." I answered slightly annoyed.

"I don't either. Besides I don't want any daddy-baby drama," the pilot said, smiling a mouth full of pearly whites.

"I am not a baby-momma drama girl!" I was really annoyed, but at the same time impressed that a man could have such beautiful teeth.

"By the way, what's your name?"

"Sarah," I replied annoyed, "What yours?"

"The plane is ready for departure," said the co-pilot as she handed the pilot some papers.

"Jim," he said writing in the corner of one of the sheet. He ripped it, "Here. Call me." Jim returned to the cockpit. I jammed his number into one of the side slots of my pocketbook, knowing that I would dump it the next time I changed my bag. But two years and three months later, Jim and I were engaged. I often reminisced about how Jim and I met. I would have never thought a simple plane ride would have resulted in finding the love of my life. We went through our checklist to make sure we were compatible. Communication was at the top of both lists. Jim had an ex-wife. He said his ex-wife had remarried and wouldn't come even if he asked. My only family member was out of the country and my parents were deceased, so Jim agreed to assist with all the wedding expenses. Jim wasn't happy that the wedding would be held in Boston. He agreed to it to make me happy. I wanted to be near my old friends.

I dialed Shanda's number, she said hello on the second ring, which caught me off guard.

"Sarah is that you?"

"Yes."

"Girl, how are you?"

"Fine, how about yourself?"

"Good!"

"I have set the date for June."

"Congratulations, I'll help you with the wedding."

"Thanks, you are just like a sister."

"Where's the wedding?"

"Boston." I said. I heard Shanda jumping up and down.

"I know the exact function room you can use, the church, the pastor…"

"Slow down, we will make all the plans next week."

"How is Jim?"

"Great."

"I am happy he is the winner." Shanda continued, "You know where to find me on Sunday mornings."

"Church." We both laughed.

Chapter Four

I arrived in Boston that Sunday morning, with Jim as the pilot.

Once arriving at Logan Airport, Jim had a return flight; I went straight to Faith Baptist Church. I took a seat in the back of the church. Late as usual. I spotted Shanda, Betty, and April sitting together up front.

Once the sermon was over and the pastor had dismissed his congregation, I waited outside. "Shanda, over here." I called. All three walked toward me, with Betty in the lead.

"Hi, Sarah," Betty said.

"Hi," I said in one gesture to all three.

"When did you get in?" April asked, as she followed the others. I thought she looked healthier than the last time I had seen her.

"This morning," I replied.

"Glad to see you at church," Betty said.

"Don't start- I know I should go more often."

"I wasn't picking at you," Betty responded.

"Sure, sure," I said.

"God finds a way to bring us back to his house," April said, laughing.

"I am leaving. Anyone wants a ride?" Betty asked.

"Drop me and Sarah off at my condo," Shanda said.

"I will not be able to join you two because I promised Eddie I would cook dinner." Betty said getting into the car.

"How is Eddie? He must miss Mary Ellen?" I asked.

"Eddie is finally getting his life back on track. He will finish his electrician apprenticeship by the end of the year." Betty said.

"That is wonderful."

"Betty got me a job with the company where she works," April said. "It's nothing great, but it keeps a roof over my head."

"That is great news." I said, "I hope that you and Betty are coming to my wedding?"

"I wouldn't miss it for the world, now that I am back on my feet."

"I would gladly come if you invite me," Betty said.

"Of course, I want you to come," I said.

The rest of the conversation was general, and not once did anyone mention Sam. So, I did.

"Sam is also invited to my wedding."

"That is fine with me," Betty said, "but Sam is the one who doesn't want to see me."

"You can't blame him," April said.

"Mary Ellen's death was horrible and I am still suffering," Betty replied.

"So is Sam." I said.

Once inside Shanda's house, she made tea. I didn't say it, but I was glad Betty and April couldn't join us. "Sarah you must stay the night," Shanda said.

"I got a hotel room reserved."

"Cancel it. Buddy went to visit his sick mother, and my baby girl is spending the night with a friend."

Since I went straight to the church from the airport I had my overnight bag. After dinner, we finalized all the wedding plans. Shanda had reserved Carol's Hall, in the heart of Roxbury. The flowers had been ordered and the menu was left up to me. Shanda had arranged for a photographer and a limo service. I was surprised that Shanda had done so much. I couldn't stop praising her. "I have to tell you the truth, so don't get mad," Shanda said.

"What is it?"

"I really didn't do it all."

I didn't say anything, because I knew exactly what she was going to say.

"You have to give most of the credit to Betty."

"I figured as much," I said.

"You're not mad, are you?"

"No, don't be silly." I was puzzled that Betty would want to help me. We relaxed on her oversized brown couch it held us both comfortably. "Where is Eddie staying these days?" I said.

"Betty moved him in with her and paid for his education. It was her way of dealing with Mary Ellen's death."

"What was the final investigator's report?"

"I promised Betty that I would let her tell you and Sam."

"Is that the reason she agreed to help with my wedding?"

"Yes."

"I figured it had to be a reason. Just tell me-she will never know?" Shanda wouldn't, so I didn't push the issue, because Shanda was a woman of her word. I know just how important that can be. My father had always said, "*A man is as good as his word.*"

I took an early flight back to Detroit the next morning.

Chapter Five

A few months before the wedding, it was too good to be true; my wedding plans were on schedule. Everyone in the wedding party was fitted and ready, except me.

Then the phone rang, I took my time answering it. I wanted to have serenity for as long as I could.

"Sarah, this is Betty."

"Betty?"

"Are you surprised to hear from me?"

"No not really," I said.

"I need to explain to you and Sam about what happened to Mary Ellen."

"Are you saying the investigation is finally over?"

"Yes, it is, thank God." Betty said, "When will you be back in Boston?"

"I will be back two days before the wedding."

"I need to talk to you and Sam the day before the wedding." Betty said.

"Have you spoken to Sam?"

"No. I was hoping you would convince him to meet with me."

"Why me?"

"Sarah, if anyone can do it, you can."

"I will do my best." I said.

"That's all I ask," Betty replied.

"Where do you want to meet?"

"We can meet at Peppers' in Cambridge at four o'clock."

"That'll work, I will talk to Sam."

After hanging up the phone, I was intrigued. What bit of information was Betty finally sharing, not because she wanted to but because she was forced. She just wanted us to hear her side of the story. My father had always said, "*There are always three sides to a story: his side, her side, and the truth lies in the middle.*"

I called Sam that very night, but he either wasn't home, or he just didn't care to answer his phone. I left a message on his answering machine for him to call me as soon as possible. I later learned he had taken a well-needed vacation.

Two weeks later, my phone rang and it was Sam.

"Sarah, what the matter?"

"Your girl, Betty, called me,"

"What did she want?"

"She wants to meet with us."

"I don't want to see her."

"I know how you feel, but I think this is important."

"Did they finish the investigation?" Sam asked.

"Yes, and she wants to share the report with us."

"Why can't she just send us the report?"

"You know Betty better than that."

"So you are saying if I want to know, I will have to see her?

"Yes."

"It seems I have no choice."

"You will have to forgive her, before moving on with your life."

"Hell, I could have raised my daughter." Sam said, not listening to me.

"I believe you. Betty had her reasons."

"They weren't good enough!"

"I am not trying to take up for her." I said, "But people who dwell in the past can't rise above their circumstances."

"I know that, but right now it hurts!"

"I can only imagine."

"Sorry, I don't want to talk any more."

Before Sam hung up, I made Sam promise to meet with Betty. Sam had a right to be bitter, but holding onto resentment would hinder his moving forward. Forgiveness is the cleanser that he will need to move on.

Chapter Six

Two days before the wedding, Jim and I came back to Boston, and stayed at the Hamlet Hotel. Having the wedding in Boston had drastically reduced the guest list to one hundred people. I was delighted that it was going to be a small wedding, which kept the cost down. "What time do you have to meet Sam and Betty?" Jim asked.

"Four."

"Well, it is three now."

"Ready. I want to see Sam before Betty arrives."

"Are you cheating on me already?" Jim asked with a smile on his face.

"Yes, one last fling."

"Just remember, I get one too."

"Okay," I said before hugging and kissing him passionately.

Jim had gone to college in Cambridge and he knew his way around the area. So, I had him drop me off at Peppers'. Sam was in the lobby at the restaurant when I arrived. As we waited for Betty, I encouraged Sam to keep his cool. "Why couldn't she just tell us over the phone?" Sam asked.

"You know Betty as well as I do. It not her style," I said.

Betty arrived, dressed in a nice blue silk dress with shoes that matched.

"Hi, I hope I didn't keep you all waiting long?"

"No" I said. Sam didn't respond.

The waitress seated us at a table in the back. She took our drink orders. I had a margarita, Sam had a double shot of bourbon, and Betty had a glass of white wine.

In an irate tone, Sam said, "Come on let's get this over with!"

"Sam, I am so sorry I hurt you, but I cannot change what happened."

"That's the problem!"

The waitress returned with our drinks, "Are you ready to order?"

"No, we are just having drinks," I said.

Betty finished her glass of wine and then said, "First of all, I want you to know that Mary Ellen's death was an accident. She had just left my house the night it happened."

"What?" Sam asked.

"Yes, she was with me that night."

"With you?" I asked.

"Yes, I tried to stop her but she wouldn't listen."

"So it was your fault!" Sam said.

Betty looked at Sam, "Someone told her before I had a chance."

"You were never going to tell her or me!" Sam exclaimed.

"That's absurd," Betty, said giving Sam a quick look and then back to an empty glass. "Let her talk," I said looking at Sam.

Betty ordered another glass of wine and started telling us what lead up to Mary Ellen's death.

"Mary Ellen and Eddie were celebrating their second year anniversary. I had rented my boss's cabin in the mountains for a week as a gift. Mary Ellen came over my house to borrow my matching luggage set. While Mary Ellen was at my house, the phone rang and the answering machine picked up. She heard the message."

"What did she hear?" Sam asked anxiously. "Sam, please this is very difficult for me." Betty said.

"It's difficult for me!" Sam continued "Get on with the story!"

"Let her talk," I said looking at Sam.

Betty's flash back of that night was vivid. She told Sam and me word for word what was said. "Mary Ellen never mentioned the call to me until she came back from the cabin," Betty said. She than turned to asked the waitress for another glass of wine.

"Get to the point!" Sam demanded.

"Mary Ellen came to my house a few days later," Betty continued, "she just started demanding answers."

"Are you my mother?" Mary Ellen asked Betty.

"Who told you that?" Betty asked Mary Ellen.

"Are you my mother?"

"I don't know what to tell you," Betty said.

"Just tell me the truth! For God sake just tell me the truth! " Mary Ellen yelled.

"Calm down, and stop using the Lord's name in vain," Betty said.

"I know you are not the one to talk to me about the Lord." Mary Ellen said with tears in her eyes, pacing back and forward."

"Just calm down."

"Did you love me?" Mary Ellen yelled.

"I gave you away, because I loved you," Betty said.

"That makes no sense." Mary Ellen replied.

"Well, I didn't think I would make a good mother."

"How would you know? You gave me away," Mary Ellen continued, "Were you ashamed of me?"

"The money I made wasn't enough. I could not provide a stable home. April and James had a stable home, money, and no children."

"Answer me! Were you ashamed of me?" Mary Ellen yelled.

"What makes you think that I would be ashamed of you," Betty replied.

"Was I not the right color baby?" asked Mary Ellen.

"Where did you hear such foolishness?"

"I overheard Aunt Shanda talking about it."

"Some of my father's people have a problem with color, but I was never like that," Betty said.

"Was that the reason?" Sam asked.

"How could you say that? My mother is black. I just look like my father who was French. When my father died my mother sent me to live with my father's family in Louisiana. My mother remarried and had Shanda and April. My mother made sure I spent the summer with my siblings."

"You three were just too close not to be sisters," Sam said.

"I never would have imagined," I said shocked with my mouth open.

Betty voice was a bit shaky but I believed she wanted to finally get the truth out in the open. She took the last swallow from her glass of wine and said, "I told Mary Ellen that she was wrong. I only allowed my sister, April, to raise her because I loved her. Mary Ellen stood still looked me in the face and said, "Who is my father?"

Betty said she didn't know what to say, so she asked Mary Ellen to give her more time. Mary Ellen said, "No more time! Who is my father?" When Betty did not give her an answer Mary Ellen's tears went out of control and she said, "I hate you for lying to me! I hate you for not taking care of me! I hate you because I lived a lie! My whole life has been a lie! If you don't tell me who my father is you will never see your (unborn) grandchild."

Betty said she grabbed Mary Ellen by her arm. She had no other recourse but to tell her Sam her godfather was her real father! Betty told us that Mary Ellen must have been hurt, disappointed, humiliated, and in shock, because she grabbed her car keys and stormed out the door crying. Betty said she wasn't able to stop her, but instead shouted, "I did it for you even if you don't believe me."

Betty said the next day she got a call from April saying that Mary Ellen car was found by the police a mile from her house. The final report stated that the wet road was the reason the car slide down the hill into the ditch hitting a tree. She had lost control.

"What was the message?" Sam demanded, "I mean the one that was left on the answering machine?"

"My paternal grandmother called to let me know she was leaving my daughter money in her will."

"What did Mary Ellen think about the message?" I asked.

"Mary Ellen didn't know what to make of the call at first, "Betty said, "That's when she went to April and asked, if I had a daughter."

"What did April tell her?" Sam asked.

"April felt it was time for Mary Ellen to know the truth. April wanted it to blow up in my face because I had denied her another loan after James' death. April wouldn't tell me that Mary Ellen was coming," said Betty.

"You should have told the truth years ago!" Sam said, his voice trembling.

"If I could, I would change what happened, but I can't! I can only ask you for forgiveness. I have accepted that I was to blame. It was my fault."

Sam looked at Betty with contempt and said, "Yes, it is your fault! You took away a part of me that I will never know and a grandchild that I will never see!" Sam stood up from the table, walked out, never looking back.

"I am so sorry," said Betty, staring at her empty glass.

I had no words for her. I stood looking down at Betty for a few seconds. I walked out of the restaurant. I hoped that Betty had learned that lies could never be a substitution for the truth.

Chapter Seven

I spent the night at Shanda's house and woke that morning to a blue sky, bluer than I had ever seen. It was the day of my wedding.

Sam arrived on time to walk me down the aisle.

"I am very happy for you, Sarah, and it's about time." Sam said.

"I love you too, Sam."

The wedding was on. Jim looked as handsome as ever.

We wrote our own vows and once the ceremony was over, all I remembered was; *"now you can kiss the bride."* A dream come true.

We walked out of the church and jumped into the limo, with the crowd blowing bubbles at us.

Jim leaned over and whispered into my ear, "I was shocked to see my ex-wife at the church."

"One of those ladies was your ex-wife?" I asked.

"Yes," Jim started to explain as I put my hand over his mouth.

"Not today" I said. "Not today."

Marriage (A-Z STORY)

At the end of twenty-five years of marriage I was, stick a fork in me, done. **B**ob hadn't had a romantic bone in his body, or acceptance of new changes. "**C**ontrol freak" was what I called him, but a good father to our kids couldn't be denied.

"**D**on't take that job; your place is in this house!" Bob's persistently demanded. **E**xcept for hosting a few dinner parties for Bob's clients, I hadn't pursued any of my goals. **F**ortunately for Bob I had put all my efforts into being a wife and mother and none into pursuing my dreams.

God blessed Bob and I with three handsome boys and one beautiful girl, which consumed our lives. **H**aving the kids in my twenties allowed me to keep up all their activities.

Invested years with Bob have left me dishearten knowing that we might be separating. **J**ust imagine, last year I was still consumed with marital rituals even after the kids moved out. "**K**eeping a roof over our heads and food on the table is my job," Bob would say. **L**ovemaking was a scheduled chore that has now been deleted.

Mislaid are my feelings for Bob now that it's just us. **N**o, I really didn't expect him to suddenly change but just admit that changes were needed. **O**utdated are the times that women are housewives and men only bring home the bacon.

Putting his needs before my own, that doesn't work for me anymore.

Quietness and serenity is what I need and someone to pick up after me. **R**espect is what I need from him for encouraging me to put my career on hold all those years. **S**omehow during my marriage I was trapped in a *bubble.* **T**he glass has burst and he sees me as the one changing and not himself as the one who needs to change.

Unfortunately we might end up in a divorce court if we can't compromise. **V**ile arguments are wearing thin what remains of our relationship. **W**hen did we stop loving each other and how can we fix it?

"**X**yana, we need to talk!" Bob yelled to me one day after one of our unnecessary disagreement about why I wouldn't pass him a near-by glass of water.

"**Y**es, we do need to talk or I will be walking right out that door!" I yelled back.

"**Z**ip it up and listen, you should be glad…!" was the last words I heard Bob say as the front door slammed behind me.

This story has 26 sentences. It was fun to write with constraints. The first sentence starts with A and the last ends in Z.

Just So You Know

Just so you know….
It's a celebration for the King.
Martin Luther King that is.

He was a man of dignity, character, and finesse,
which made people take notice, even the press.

His writings had wisdom of insights,
defending our civil rights.

His speeches inspirited a world to change,
where blacks no longer felt ashamed.

His selfless acts opened his life to attacks,
protecting human rights for women and blacks.

Just so you know…
It was the wickedness that took him away,
but his dreams are here to stay,
they can never be driven astray.

With the power of God's grace,
we were given another to take his place.
A man born of both race.

Just so you know…
Barack Obama is his name.
A name that brought no shame,
to a world that needed change.

A true vision of King's dream detected.
Obama was the one we selected,
with black and white votes he was elected.

His goals are the same as King's..
to give voice to the poor,
and keep America jobs on this shore.

Yes we did it!
We knew we could,
and it was Martin Luther King
who said we would.

Just so you know…

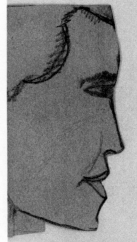

Willie Pleasants, Poet
© 2009

IS IT ME?

Is it me? Or have American companies outsourced all of its customer service agents? It seems that some of the people answering the phone accents are so thick that only every fifth word is recognizable. And for the others, "Hello may I..." is the only thing that can be understood. The folk who provide that service is supposed to assist the customers not frustrate them.

Well in the effort to be a Good Samaritan I tried to endure the pain of the **800** numbers to help my aunt. I was calling them to find out why my aunt hadn't received her investment check.

"Are you speaking English?" I asked the customer service lady on the phone.

"I'm speaking good English," the lady on the phone said.

Well, after the third time asking, "What did you say?" I requested (jokingly) to be transferred to an agent in the United State who spoke broken English.

Finally they transferred me to someone I could understand, and service was about to be had.

"My aunt, Kay Smith, Account #22222 has not received her check, and I would like to know why?" I asked.

Of course they take all the information needed, and then they put me ON HOLD. I had to listen to that elevator music that should be calming but instead the outdated tunes made me angry.

The lady returned to the phone and told me, "The check has been cashed."

"By who?" I continued, "My Aunt said she never received the check."

"There is nothing we can do. The check has been cashed," she said.

"My aunt is on a fixed income and needs her money to pay rent," I said with an elevated tone determined to help my aunt.

"The only other thing we can do is get a copy of the check," she said.

"How long will that take?" I asked with no patience.

"A week," she said.

"That's just too long! She is an elderly person who needs her money. We need to resolve this as soon as possible!" I must have been yelling at that point because she told me to calm down. She would work on it herself and get back to me in a few days.

She was a woman of her word; within a few days a copy of the cancelled check came in the mail and guess whose signature was on it? Yes, my aunt.

POEMS FOR EVERYONE

FROM WILLIE PLEASANTS' COLLECTION

Goals

Sitting on the ground looking around
does no good if your goals can't be found.
You got to have a goal to hold your ground,
that's what makes you strong and sound.

A goal helps you stay on top of your game.
It helps you play, and still maintain.
It helps you know where you are.
It helps you shine like a natural bright star.

FREE

Jail is not for me
I need to spread my limbs like a tree

I need freedom close at sight
So I can have a good sleep at night.

Jail is not for me,
That not where I need to be, right?
Being black is hard enough without that fight.

Jail is not for me---I need to be FREE!!
To grow and enjoy life's liberties.

Crabs

I reached down to lend you a hand.
To help you with your plan.
You quickly closed your eye
and took no stand.

Then:
I reached down to offer you my plan,
Instead… you pulled me in,
turned your back and ran.

Father's Day

We came to spread gratitude your way,
We ask God to bless your earthly stay,

We want to acknowledge you on this day
By taking all your chores away,
No long hours of work, just play.
And **Thanking You** is what we came to say.

Thank you,
For fighting the battles that won the wars
Which saved lives, with promises of a few gold stars.

Thank you,
For harvesting the fields
which created the meals
that kept your family stomachs filled.

Thank you,
For taming the beast
And bring home freedom's feast.

Thank you,
For raising your son to be a man,
because no woman can.

Thank you,
For teaching your daughters to be respected
Without being neglected.

Thank you,
For being that one of a kind,
and serving you today is clearly on our mind.

We want to say **Thank you** again,
For being the men **God** created close to his heart,
and in his image men should not dodge,
Because they are truly the earthly **Fathers** - he left in charge.

Shoebox Dream

There it was, I had found
Encased in a box painted with a clown.
It belongs to my mother, I once said with a frown,
Full of contemplated memories just lying around.

I believed it held dreams that could have been,
if mother had not veered off-track into sin.
Her youth and ambition had died then,
leaving her confused, and bewildered in the end.

My mother's sadness caused my heart to tear,
because my mother's time on earth had stopped here.
With her forsaken dreams dead between her ears,
She left me a note that said:
"With love, I leave you this box, My Dear."

Flipping through her papers and pictures were not fun,
pieces of her childhood dreams undone.
I was left depressed, doleful, and stunned,
that she might not connect with God's bond.

With the shoebox, and aspirations of her dreams,
Retuning her to the earth was harder than it seemed.
May she now dwell within a spiritual serene,
as her ashes float down a clear water stream.

August 8, 2000

No place to hide

He sees from on high
He lives out there beyond the sky

God is the one who sees all,
Let him be the one you call.

Like a ship in rough tide
He can be your guide.

He will count your deeds
And supply all your needs.

Dr. Jen

Dr. Jen's powerful advise that can save a life:

If you have a cold, feed your soul.
If you have gas and it will not pass,
take mustard and a pickle and it won't last.

Colon cleansers are your friends,
they will purify your inner-skin.

Exercising will extend your life,
you might even out-live your wife.

Reading and problem solving stimulates your mind
It helps you to be sane and fine.

Father to Son

I am your father, my son.
Stay close to my teaching until I am done.

I will guide you the right way,
teach you not to stray.
For the world can be a cruel playground to play,
when evil threaten any good day.

I will teach you to be calm,
to follow your own mind and sing your own song.

I will teach you to love you,
and help you stay true.
Without stepping on another's shoe.

Take my hand, my son.
With God's words, his will be done.

My Name

Call me by my name.
I am not a shame.
It always the same.

I am not a bitch…
I am not a whore…
I will not accept those names any more.

So, whenever you see me
Call me by my name
It's the same, my name

It not a game
It's My Name!

Teachers

They speak words and do not mutter.
Open minds, and clears away children's clutter.

They lay the foundation for a young mind,
to function in society helping mankind.

Love

This poem is for you with a smile
I haven't told you I love you in awhile.
I Love you!!

Beulah's Song (Ocean Blue)

In desperation, I jumped in my car,
I drove faster than a shooting star,
hoping to liberate my mind of iron bars.

Driving with strong emotions,
guided with a stress free notion,
of being on the beach facing the ocean.

Stopping briefly along the way,
admiring the old oak trees of yesterday.
With their moss filled limps of gray.

Like garland on Christmas trees in May.
The Oak trees formed a beautiful archway,
lifted my spirits and made me want to stay.

Continuing to the dolphin swimming near the shore,
To the sunset at my backdoor,
and to the lure of the ocean sounds once more.

Weekend Trip

Imagine me on my way home
Riding the rails
tired as hell
Traveling on a four engine train
Three of which has failed.

I was stuck on that train that wouldn't go
which had too many stops, and went too slow.
Two hours had turned into four.
I was ready to walk through the door,
OFF that train and back home once more.

TO YOU (Nat)

I wrote this poem,
if you were blue,
to let you know my thoughts are with you.

I wrote this poem,
because of the beauty I see inside,
brighter than an angel's halo unable to hide.

God's love will protect, and forever be your guide.
You are an earthly warrior who stands at his side.

Don't worry; your body will heal in time,
Relax, enjoy, and rest your mind,
You have done all you can; it's God's time to shine.

Ghetto Girl

She is a Ghetto girl from around the way
Who really don't know why she strayed.
She has never learned any other way.
She is a wild child with plenty of play.

She likes to do her hair with a tint
She lives in a development because of the rent,
with a child that's the hint.
She spends her free time on the telephone line,
talking to her friends on someone else's dime.

She should stop hanging out late at night,
being around men who fight,
they're guaranteed to help loose her rights.
She needs to stay away from those so call friends.
And learn how to play the game to WIN.

Election

The election drummers has got me bound,
using ignorance to make a touchdown.
They hope our common sense is
in the lost and found.

They spread their evil out to take hold
of the good citizens who should be in control.
Ain't it a shame when thing can't change
Being Black is still a racial card game.

People get a grip start denouncing rhetoric.
The important issues in life should not be
whether they are black or white.
But what happens when we try entering the door,
the code has changed and it exist no more.

Oil is high and gas price is escaping.
The war that never should have started
with no sign of ending.
We are not safe in our home,
if we need cameras on every telephone.

They waste our time and promised us a peace of mind.
Give us false hope about bring our troops home.
They give us an extra refund and tax it like a loan.
But when it all finally the end,
and the electoral are gone.
May the best person inherit the throne.

Dawn's Song

Your visions are strong and deep.
Hidden inside within your reach.
Your unrealized dreams will not sleep.
They are yours not to keep.
So, open your eyes and make that leap.

Day for the Heart

Some say:
Valentine day…. what's the deal?
It just another day for the dollar bills.
For hugs, kisses, and candy, if you will.

Others say:
It's a day for lover's heart,
to come together if they are apart.

I say:
It's a day to forgive and forget,
which makes it the best day yet.

LEGACY

Planting your feet firmly on the ground,
                Allows your mind to move around.
                Focus on your life's spots,
Pick your legacy's plot,
Careful at picking your stops.
Never give up!!!
        Till you reach the top.

Women's History

There is no mystery about women history.
Women are the other creation of mankind,
Who were expected to just walk behind,
have babies, cook, and never use their minds.

For years women have been discriminated against,
Even been denied the same opportunities as men.
But, it wasn't long before they changed their roles,
Became bold, and struggled for more of life's control.

Women like Sojourner Truth who changed the world
by leading a multitude of slaves to freedom.
Women like Susan B. Anthony who did lot of things to
support our social justice fight.
Women like Rosa Parks who fought for civil rights for black.
Women like Elizabeth Stanton who spoke out for
women's voting rights.

It is important to note that women can accomplish
anything when they put their minds to it.
They have done some amazing things and need
to be respected and appreciated.

For, if there were no women the world would not change.
If there were no women the earth would be strange.
If there were no women there would be more strife.
If there were no women there would be no life!

Composed by
Fifth Graders of Mason Middle School
Written by Willie Pleasants, Poet
April 20, 2008

ABOUT THE AUTHOR

This is the author's second book of short stories and spiritual poems. She loves sharing her experience with others. She hopes that her stories and poems will continue to offer inspiration, enjoyment, and the knowledge that life and living must go on even with adversities.

The author has included at the end of this book a showcase of collaborated stories, poems, blogs and personal testimonials by a group of inspiring writers. She is honored that they have allowed her the opportunity to include their works in her book. She hopes you will enjoy them as well.

Keep the faith and Make Truth a Habit...

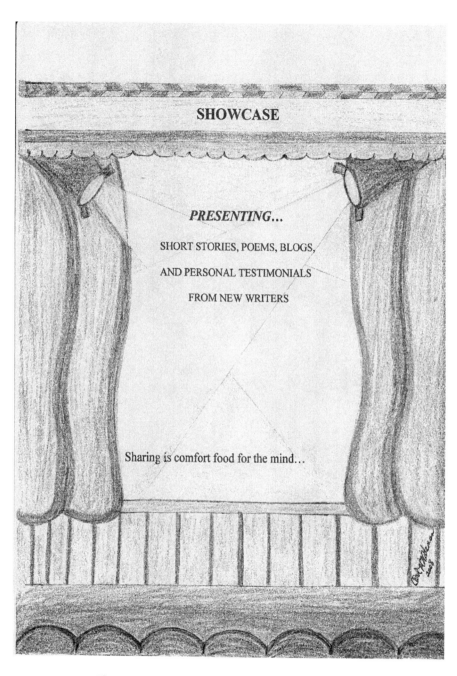

Showcase stage drawing by Carol Wideman

Father Have Mercy

For every eye that sheds a tear
Father have Mercy and draw them near.

For every hand that reaches out in need.
Father have mercy and send an angel to sow a seed.

For every ear that's able to hear.
Father have mercy and anoint a messenger to preach without fear.

For every sin, for everyone, Father have mercy,
It is finished, it is done.

For every body beat, worn and torn
Father have mercy, that's why Jesus was born.

For the weak, be strong, Father have mercy.

Open their eyes, so they may see

Hold on to their hands and make them free.

Let your word be heard.

Heal their bodies and save the lost, that's why Jesus died on the cross.

Father have mercy, thank you for your Grace.

Written by: Glory Wideman

MY FEELING ON LIFE

Born in a small town in Alabama I was raised by my grandmother after my mother married. My grandmother refused to allow me to live with my mother. My grandmother decided it was best for all concerned. So, there I was left at the age of three to be molded by her. I called her "mama," she taught me how to survive and live a good Christian life.

I was taught to cope with everyday tasks by reading the Bible and talking to God. At the age of eight a miracle happened in my life, or maybe just a pivotal moment that made me believe in God.

I had an annoying roaring in my ear. I went to my grandmother and told her about the sound, and she said,

"Pray to God for healing, because we live to far in the woods to get to a doctor on feet."

My grandmother also explained that there was no money to spare for doctor visits. I think there was only one old doctor in town. So, I took her advice and got the Bible and sat outside on the porch. I read, and read and prayed and prayed for the roaring to go away. It finally did and never returned. That day I realized that God was very real. He may not come when you want him, but he is right on time.

I didn't always follow everything that was taught to me, but that training has kept me grounded. *The Bible states a person must do these things to enjoy life and have many happy days.*

We should stop and reflect on life's occurrences for which we have no control like the weather, life, and death. There must be a God and we need our children to be exposed to his power, so they can have someone to believe in.

With all the shooting, robbing, and bombing in the world, we all need God in our lives. I am not trying to push my belief onto anyone. I wanted to share my earlier experience about God.

I have a deep love for my family and a respect for my friends. God and my family always come first. Friends with attitudes come and go, but God will be there for life.

Written by: Jeannette Johnson 2008

BEZ'S BLOG

I just want to know who is responsible for this mess. Love, honor, obey, cherish, till death due us part? Get real man! We are the most imperfect creatures on the planet. Why are we trying to live up to the unrealistic expectation called marriage? I think it's time for some new rules. The human heart has room for lots of love (and I am not talking about sex here). I think we were meant to enjoy this life. Infidelity is becoming the norm these days. Here is my solution to help stamp out this plague with some new rules for this thing called marriage.

1. There should be a six months waiting period before marriage once you obtain license. (I 'm sure this will weed out a whole lot of fools)
2. If either party has children, waiting period is one year even if you were not married before.
3. Marriage is only valid for 5 years. At the end of that time couples can chose to renew or be on their way. Separation is possible if you don't survive the 5 years but you cannot remarry until the 5 years are up. Prenuptial agreements are required even if you don't have a dime. Courts can intervene and handle issues not covered by the penults. Death of a spouse cannot invalidate the validity period. (So you can't bump off your mate to get out of it.)

At the end of the first 5 years if you choose to renew, you must renew every 10 years until death. A new prenuptial must be signed each time you renew.

This can eliminate the need for so many divorces; unfortunately, it won't eliminate the need for lawyers, because we can still screw up a whole-lotta-shit. Lets take some of pressure off ourselves. Mate for life!

Written by: Beulah Meyers 2008

WHEN YOU ARE SAVED

Sue was sitting on the side of her bed when the doctor called and said,

"You may not live to see the month out."

"I worked all my life to have a good home for my family. I had hoped to live long enough to see all my six children grown. I have a good husband for whom I tried to do right by. I go to church every Sunday. I visited the sick and paid my tithes in the church. Taught all my children to pray and believe in God. God is the heavenly father they must keep his commandments just like we all must do for our earthly fathers," said Sue at the age of forty-eight. Sue tried to contain her emotion as her sister entered the room.

"What's the matter?" Molly asked. Sue told her sister what the doctor had just told her. Molly was devastated to hear that her baby sister was dying.

"What should I do now?" Sue asked Molly.

"You have to be strong." Molly said.

"I 'm not ready to die."

"I don't want you to die, but death is not a decision for us to make."

"I'm starting to have doubts about being saved," Sue said.

"Have you not been born again of the spirit and baptized?

"Yes"

"Has the spirit not hit you?"

"I don't know."

"Did you shout, mourn, or feel something?

"I just don't know, but I hope that I'm saved."

"You have to know before you die. You have to pray to God. You must ask him to show you that you are saved."

"You are right sister. I had forgotten for a second that it is about God and faith."

"The very second you believe that you are saved you don't have to hope any more. You will know it." Molly said as her sister prayed.

Written by: M. Wideman

My Feeling

My heart is broken

and my spirit don't feel so good right now.

I feel my family is broken up because

my Mom and brother are in one house and

I am living with my Nana. I go home on the weekend.

My cousin moved to Arizona and I will pray that one day

we can all come together and be a family again.

I know that God answer prayers. My Nana told me that

a family that pray together stays

TOGETHER.

HAPPY MOTHER'S DAY

Written by Dimera L. Capel Wideman

2005

Age 10

MY RECOVERY

We all have had experiences that have molded our future. I had the unfortunate burden to have to live through one that was thrust upon me.

I was born in the south at a time when a child was told, "a child should be seen and not heard." A child was considered disrespectful if they "talked back to adults".

To talk about sex was also taboo. Sex was something that people did and didn't talk about at all. I am not saying this happen in every home, but the ones I grew up around.

Being inquisitive, I always wanted to know why? Once I heard my mother talking to her sister-in-law about a young girl in the streets whose mother allowed her to date an older man. My mother said, "Before you know it she will make out with him and get pregnant. She will have a baby out of wedlock and will never do anything with her life." I was six years old when I heard this and I wanted to know what was making out. What did making out have to do with having a baby? So I asked my mother those questions only to be told, "You are too young to be noising in grown folk's business." My mother told me never to ask her any question about what she was talking about on the phone. I was told that a child should stay in a child's place. She told me to stop asking her questions that had nothing to do with me. She also told me that when I get older she would explain to me where babies came from and what making out is. I am sure she was only telling me the same thing her mother had told her.

Well, sadly to say my first introduction about sexuality was rape. I was raped at the age of six by a neighbor across the street from our family house while living in the south. He said, "If you tell anyone what I did to you, I will kill you." I ended up keeping the secret. No matter how I tried I couldn't get rid of the feel of the rapist hand touching my body, and his voice out of my head. I thought that keeping this secret would mean it would never come back to show its ugly face. Then I was repeatedly raped again by a relative at the age of ten to fourteen while living in the north. He said the same words that the first rapist used.

By this time I had developed fear, guilt, mistrust, low self-esteem, and the sleepless nights. Unknowingly this had caused me to never want to know are gaining any insight into normal sexuality. I had come to feel that a man takes what he wants from you and leaves you in fear of your life. Even when my breasts started to develop, hair under my arm, and having my menstrual period (and this might sound stupid), but I believed that these changes came about because I got raped. I further felt shame, because I thought it was my fault.

My family told me that they loved me I could not trust them. I grew up believing that my family and friends were very loving and caring, but two people that I felt I should have been able to trust raped me. This made it even harder to get pass the mistrust, anger and pain. I feared being judged. I felt as if I was the only one who had experienced being raped. I responded to this event by shutting everyone out of my life. I felt that no one would understand what I was going through. I was feeling anger and fear. I didn't know how to express my feelings and my emotions. I often wanted to tell someone what had happened to me. I just didn't think anyone would believe me. So, the birds and bees discussion never happened.

After many years of my life spiraling out of control with drugs and a baby, I had finally hit rock bottom. I knew my fear and pain would not get any better until I had peace in my heart. For many years, I was not able to find a breakthrough because the rape had been suppressed.

Living in a shelter with a child after losing my apartment where my rent was only $40 a month. Hitting rock bottom was truly an eye opener.

My breakthrough actually came during my drug abuse counseling. As I analyzed my drug addiction, I was able to uncover the pain that I had suffered from the rape. During my intervention I had came to terms with the rape not being my fault. There are some sick people out there in the world. It was not my fault! I was finally able to forgive my rapist by writing painful letters on how they had hurt me. I would love to have been able to face them and ask them why me? But unfortunately they are dead.

This is my story and I hope it will help others in their recovery. Over the years, the root of my self-destructive behavior was the result of being exposed to sexual abuse at an early age. Drugs were used as a way to escape the memory of my past and created illusions of comfort. These illusions of comfort lead to an association with negative people and eventually serving time in prison. My faith says "the truth shall set you free," and my therapist said, "Healing begins with talking and being honest."

Once I was able to open up and confess what had happen and the earth didn't fall out of the sky, I knew that it was well with the Lord.

God is good and good is God.   I have been drug free for sixteen years. I stay grounded in the word.   I am more open with my children by keeping open dialogs with them, about them, and about their lives.   I have completed my Culinary Arts Degree.   I am working on opening up my own catering company.

Written by: Sandra G. Wideman   June 2008

TELL ME THAT YOU CARE

WHISPER IN MY EAR, TELL ME THAT YOU CARE

SHOW ME THAT YOU LOVE ME, ONLY IF YOU DARE

SAY THE THINGS I WANT TO HEAR, ONLY IF THEY'RE TRUE

LIES WILL BRING US PROBLEMS AND MAKE ME FEEL SO BLUE

MAKE OUR TIME TOGETHER AS SPECIAL AS CAN BE

AND I WILL KNOW YOU MEAN IT, FOR I'LL FEEL YOUR LOVE FOR ME

HAPPY WE WILL BE FOREVER AND A DAY

WE'LL SHOW EVERYONE WE KNOW HOW OUR LOVE JUST LIGHTS THE WAY

AND SOMEDAY WHEN ONE OF US IS GONE AND BROKEN IS OUR HEART

WE'LL LIVE ON LOVELY MEMORIES CREATED FROM THE START

THEN ONE DAY WHEN WE MEET AGAIN IN THE GREAT AND VAST BEYOND

WE'LL ALWAYS BE WITH ONE ANOTHER AND NEVER AGAIN SAY SO LONG

Written by: Denis DeOliveira

THE MESSAGE

Zack's teenage years are quickly passing like a speeding train that passes through a station without stopping. Hattie diligently uses every available moment to pass on all her life's experiences and relative's accomplishments and failures. A male mentor was assigned to help Zack see himself as a productive man. Spiritual teachings were in the box of things to learn before he leaves home.

"Zack, before you know it the time will come for you to move on," said Hattie.

"I know," said Zack, "I remember all the important lessons, but some of the advice is kind of a waste of time."

"Be careful not to throw out good information just because you think it's a waste of time," Hattie said in an effort to prepare him for living on his own.

"He's a teenager" she thought to herself, this is normal.

"The teachers are making us work on spelling and penmanship," said Zack one morning while getting dressed for school, "I don't see why we need to. I can do the work better on the computer."

"Are you now smarter than the teachers?" Hattie asked.

"I don't bother reading the instructions because I know it's the same old stuff I had before," said Zack.

"If it's being taught, you should take the time to learn it. You never know, you may need it one day." Hattie said.

Hattie remembered being told by a friend, Loren, "If you want them to learn something you got to trick them into thinking it was their idea." Hattie told Loren that she didn't approve of using tricks to teach good values to children.

Loren told this story to Hattie and suggested that she tell it to Zack, so Hattie did.

There was a young man, educated with a good job, on his way to succeed with all that he thought he needed. One day, little sparks had gotten on the back of his coattail. He quickly brushed them aside, thinking this is nothing, no problem and continued on with his daily life.

An elder co-worker, who had many years on the job saw the little sparks and warned the young man to put them out. "Take heed, my man; take care of the sparks before they get bigger and out of control." As time passed the young man's life got busy and he didn't notice the sparks had gotten bigger and had become a small fire.

For you see, the little sparks were the forgotten lessons learned that the young man threw out. He thought he knew it all and the elder co-worker had nothing to teach him. His procrastination had taken hold and projects were doomed for failure. His career went down in flames.

Hattie hoped that the story would help Zack see what can happen if he continues to think he knows everything and choose to ignore creditable people with good advice. She had instilled in him faith, love and personal values and wondered how much of this Zack would apply to his own life to make good life choices.

"So, Zack what do you think of my story?" Hattie asked.

"Huh" said Zack, with a curious look, "I'll give it some thought."

Written by: Carol M.Wideman 2008

Untitled

People and Cars directions are the same.
The decisions in their lives are
determined on their choice of lanes.

Written by: Mareese M. Wideman, Jr. 2008

The Encounter

I was reading Genesis 32:22-32 on April 7th and 8th, the story of Jacob wrestling with God.

On April 9th, my cell phone alarm went off at 3:33 a.m. I hadn't set it. As I looked around the bedroom, I started to think about the story of Jacob. I got out of my bed and started to pray to God to bless me, my family, friends and whoever I come in contact with daily. I didn't pray very long.

On April 10th, my cell phone alarm went off again at the same time. 3:33 a.m. I stared at the time and I looked around the bedroom. Again, I started to think about the story of Jacob. I got out of bed and kneeled down beside it and pray and worship God longer than the night before.

I remembered having a limp (left leg) as I was walking around the room praying. I also remember thinking "I do not see anyone in the room." Good, because that would have scared the life out of me.

I know God was there in the room with me because I felt safe and content. I did not feel fearful or scared. The next morning the pain in my leg was gone.

Each of the nights I thought I was wrestling with God. But God was wrestling with me. I was looking for a personal encounter with God and I got it.

Thank God for answering my prayer.

Written by: Dorothy Wideman   2008

My Mother's Struggle

She prayed and did her best to keep it all together.
And with God blessing her,
Kept the lights on.
And paid the rent.

She was able to pay all her bills,
and still put on the table all the meals.

Taught each child so they wouldn't fail.
Made sure we went to school and not to jail.

When school let out, we all had fun
playing down in Florida's hot sun.

By: Leshawn Wideman   2008
At age 10

Freedom!!!

"See, this is what we are going to do. We are going through the woods to get to Lexington. When we get there, we wait until midnight. The second it hit midnight we will do an all out ambush against the British." said Mr. Barry.

"Excellent plan Sir," replied Blue.

These were the colonists making an attack on the British on Christmas day. This plan was excellent, in fact, BRILLIANT because they never fight at night or fight on the holidays. The colonist had three organizers. The three organizers of the colonist were Paul Barry, Willy Johnson, and Blue. They were all good men, who wanted to fight this war because they believed there was no other way to make the British stop taxing them, making rules for them and to listen to their requests for change.

Paul Barry was a nice man. He had a wife and two kids. His wife helped the colonist by making food and clothing. He was the one who made up all the plans they did against the British. He was their leader in charge. Willy Johnson, on the other hand, had a girlfriend. She helped Mr. Barry's wife with food. He leads the colonist into battle. Blue was different. No one knew what his last name was. He had no wife. He only had a girlfriend, who dumped him when he got involved in the war. Blue was a spotter. Blue looked out to see if he saw any red coats, and gave the sign, "the British are coming!" He is the one always putting his two-cents in.

"So, we move in an hour?" Willy Johnson asked.

"Yes Sir!!!" Mr. Barry said.

"We should get some sleep," said Blue.

"You're right, we need a half an hour sleep," said Mr. Barry.

Everyone went to bed and the leaders got their half an hour of sleep. The three leaders got up and got prepared for war. The colonists woke up at eleven o'clock. They all got ready for war and to march to Lexington. When they got to Lexington it was eleven-thirty o'clock. So they waited, and waited, and waited. It was eleven-fifty eight o'clock. They woke the others that had fallen asleep.

"On my count," said Willy Johnson, "Five, Four, Three, Two, One… GO, GO, GOOOOOOOOOOO!!!!!"

The colonists ran to the first house and shot in it, but no one was in that house. The British came out of hiding to see what all the noise was. They didn't know that they were being ambushed. When the colonists saw the British they opened fire. The colonists and the British fought for hours. The British retreated and the colonists finally won that battle after four hours of fighting. All the colonists went to Concord to regroup. All accept Blue.

They didn't know, but Blue had gotten shot four times in four different places in his leg.

"AHHHH!!!!!! The pain!!!!!!!!!! It hurts," said Blue.

All the noise he was making attracted the British. He started crawling back to Concord.

The British made up a quick plan.

"We should follow this guy, and I'll bet you he will lead us back to the colonists!"

"Yeah that's a good plan, but let's give him his space."

So that is what the British did. Blue didn't know that the British were following him. He was crawling back to safety; he thought that he was going to die out in the woods. One night he even had to sleep in the woods. The British was still following him. The colonists were celebrating their victory and they didn't even miss him until the next day.

The next day, Willy Johnson, and Paul Barry were making another plan to wipe out the rest of the British.

"This is what we are going to do," said Mr. Barry, "we are going to use Bunker Hill to our advantage. We are going to stay on the top of the hill and wait until the British come and that is when we surprise their asses and wipe them out"

"That is a good idea," said Willy, "What time do we leave?"

"Hey wasn't Blue suppose to tell me how good of a plan that was, where is he?"

"I don't know! I never saw him after we left for Concord!"

"OH MY GOD!!!!!!!!!!! Do you think he is dead?"

"I can't say Sir, but we need to look for him first thing in the morning!!!!!!"

Blue wasn't even half way back to Concord. He woke up with more pain in his leg then he had before. It felt like someone was poking at it. The British were still following him. He started crawling again. The blood was still coming out of his leg but faster than ever. Blue tried to crawl faster but he couldn't. It was around six o'clock in the evening and he was still in the woods but closer to the village than he was last night. He kept crawling. He was in pain. He kept crawling and crawling. He never gave up. He wanted to live to see another day. So he kept crawling. Then Blue heard a twig break.

"What was that?" Blue stuttered.

"What the hell, pick up your feet," one of the British whispered, "He is the only one that can lead us to the colonists."

Blue realized that the British were following him and they were using him to trap the colonists.

"Blue... Blue... Blue, Where are you Blue?" shouted Willy Johnson!

"Did you have any luck finding Blue?" said Mr. Barry.

"No Sir," said Willy, "We have everyone looking for him."

Blue comes out the woods screaming to the top of his voice, "RUNNNNNNNNNNNNN!!!!!"

"Hey, there he- BANG!!!!!"

"RUNNNNNN!" Blue shouted, "RUNNN-BANG"

Blue was shot in the back. Blue died right then and there.

THE BRITISH ARE HERE EVERYONE FIGHT BACK!!!! FIGHT FOR YOUR   LAND!!!!FIGHT FOR YOUR RIGHTS!!!!!" said Mr. Barry.

Every one of the colonists fought until they had no more ammunition. A lot of the colonists died right there. When the British did a body count, there were a hundred and fifty dead bodies lying there, but only three were the British. The colonists had to retreat and go somewhere else, which was Bunker Hill.

"How can Blue do this to us!" said Willy Johnson.

"He didn't," said Mr. Barry. "Didn't you hear him screaming run before he got shot! He was a spotter, but also my friend."

"How can we get the British back for what they did to Blue?" Willy Johnson asked.

"Honestly, I don't know," Mr. Barry said, "I truly don't know."

"Listen to yourself man; you lead us to many victories and defeats against the British. You have to make up a plan, you got to!!!" said Willy.

"Okay we are going with the same plan, but different strategy!" said Mr. Barry. "This is what we are going to do."

So, the next day every one of the colonists that had survived last night's tragedy went to Bunker Hill. They had someone go to the British and lead them to Bunker Hill. A decoy went to the village where the British were staying and got them to follow him back to Bunker Hill.

"Hey you guys!" the colonist said. "How is your day?"

"A colonist!!" shouted the British, "GET HIM!!!"

The colonist ran. The British ran after him. He ran his heart out. He ran, and ran, and ran. The British was about a mile away but they could still see him. They finally got to Bunker Hill. He ran to the top of the hill.

"The British are coming," he said to Mr. Barry, out of breath, "They are coming up the hill right now!"

"On my count," said Willy, "THREE... TWO... ONE... GO... GO... GO... GO... OPEN FIRE!!!!!!"

When Willy said open fire the colonist ran to the edge of the hill and open fire on the British. There were way more British than the colonists. The colonists made that observation, but still fought back. They fought, and fought back until the British was closer to them then they could imagine. So they had to retreat again. They retreated with dignity and pride. They went back to the village and everybody got some sleep. The British on the other hand didn't. The British realized that they would have to take the colonists serious from now on. They mean business.

"The colonists are much stronger than they use to be," said one of the British soldier.

"Don't be silly, they can't beat us. They don't even have a uniform on their backs like us." said another.

"They clearly whooped our asses with belts they don't even have. We need to take the colonists more seriously now." said the British soldier. "We can't play around with them like we use to. They have more weapons; they have more ammunition than we do. We need to fight this like this is a real war so we won't get our asses beat like that again!"

Back at the colonists village Willy Johnson and Mr. Barry had a conversation while everyone else was sleeping.

"We did a number on the British, didn't we?" asked Willy Johnson, "we whooped their asses like our mothers use to beat ours!!! Good night, Sir."

"Good night." said Mr. Barry, "See you in the morning."

Mr. Barry stayed up for a little while longer. When he was about to go to bed he heard a knock on the door. He opened the door. At the door was a young man.

"Hi Sir, I was wondering if my father is here" said the young man.

"Who is your father?" asked Mr. Barry, strangely.

"Blue Rooty-to-Booty, Sir"

"What is your name young man?"

"Snap Rooty-to-Booty, Sir."

"I'm sorry to tell you this but-"

"My father is dead, I know."

"How did you know that?"

"I saw his body lying out in the first village I went to, to look for you guys." Snap said, "I wanted to know if I can join the war on your side. I will follow every instruction that you give me, and I can-"

"Woo, slow down buddy, slow down. My name is Mr. Barry and you can fight with us against the British. You will take your father's place as spotter. You will meet everybody tomorrow morning. Get some sleep and I'll wake you up at eight o'clock. Okay Snap?"

"OKAY!!!!" said Snap, "and Mr. Barry."

"Yes." said Mr. Barry,

"Just call me Rooty-to Booty".

"Yes Sir!" said Mr. Barry, "Good night Rooty-to-Booty."

Rooty-to-Booty took over his father's spot in the war. Rooty-to-Booty was happy about taking his father's spot, but Mr. Barry was happy about something else. He was happy because he found out his best friends' last name.

"Rooty-to-Booty... Rooty-to-Booty... Rooty-to-Booty... that was his last name. "Rooty-to-Booty. I finally know his last name," said Mr. Barry to himself.

"I need to get some rest so I can introduce Rooty-to-Booty to everyone tomorrow morning."

The next morning Mr. Barry woke everyone up early to meet Blue's son, Snap. When everyone gathered around outside, Mr. Barry started talking.

"Everybody this is Blue's son, Snap." said Mr. Barry. "He would like to be called Rooty-to-Booty. He will be taking his father spot as a spotter. I want everyone to give Rooty-to-Booty a warm welcome into the colonists group and into the war."

Rooty-to-Booty came to replace his father and help continue the struggle against the British for taxing the colonists, unfair rules and a ruler who didn't want to listen.

Everyone gave Rooty-to-Booty a warm welcome. Rooty-to-Booty felt welcomed. After that first hour of welcoming, the three leaders went straight to business. They made a new plan of how they were going to wipe out the British completely so they would not have to see them again.

"This is the plan. We have an all-out ambush. We just go to the village and go all-out," said Mr. Barry. Mr. Barry was back to his old self again. He was making new plans.

"I don't think we have to go to the village!" said Rooty-to-Booty while grapping his weapon, "the war is coming to us."

"Everybody got their weapons and went into hiding. They saw the British. They were not that many this time."

"On my count," said Willy Johnson. "ONE... TWO... THREE... OPEN FIRE!!!!!!!!"

The colonists came out of hiding and went all out. They fired, then reloaded, then fired again. They fought the war like it was their last day of living. When they killed all the British in that area they went to the village that the British took over and did a clean sweep and made sure that there were no more British soldiers left. The colonists finally won. They won the war. They had beaten the British. They celebrated as soon as the last British soldier was reported dead. They had beer and a party. Mr. Barry, Willy Johnson, and Rooty-to-Booty all had earned three stripes: Pride, Dignity, and Respect. They were the leaders of the colonists and they fought other wars after that. They all fought until their death. These colonists were real honorable men!!!

Written by: Christopher D. Andrews Wideman
March 2008
Age 16

Coleman

Birth to parents determine by God's direction. Angels were given to him for his protection.

Birth and sculptured for a specific design, this male child was one of a kind.

Arriving on earth on July 21, 1925, so full of love, determination, and a strong will to survive.

Birth with a mission for battle to fight in World War II, He was celebrated.

A cook and gunman he was decorated.

Behold a maturing man steps into a wonderful life, having ten great children and just one wife.

A man full of humor and "Have You's." Raised us up early to lay down a foundation of Godly morals and values.

Aged and baptized transformed his mind in many ways. His spiritual wisdom is what we live by today.

A man three score and almost ten left this world, yet that's not the end.

He's in heaven SAVED and VICTORIOUS. The fight he fought was WON and it was GLORIOUS.

Written by: Vickie Wideman-Victor   2008

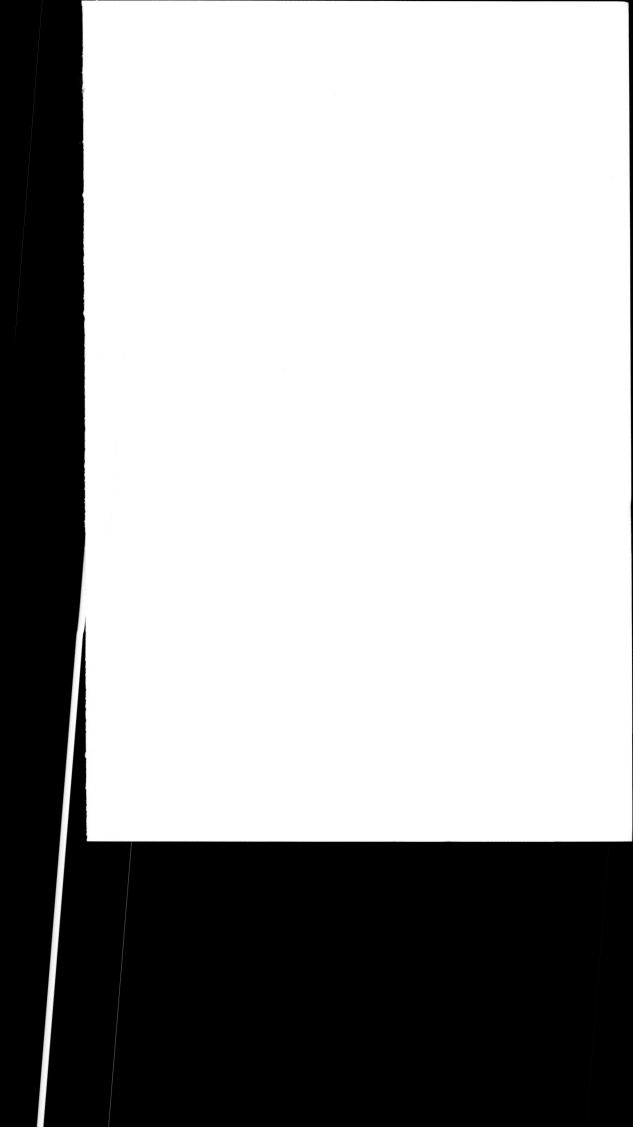

Breinigsville, PA USA
11 October 2010
247140BV00001B/6/P

9 781438 930053